Triumphing Through My Dyslexic World

A Servant Advocate in the Marketplace

Marlon Harmon

Triumphing Through My Dyslexic World
By Marlon Harmon

Edited by LLVE, LLC: Dr. Yvette Rice
Cover Design by Jan Hammond
Typesetting by Inktobook.com
Published by Amanda Goodson Global, LLC

Printed in the United States of America
ISBN: 978-1-951501-21-1
eBook ISBN: 978-1-951501-22-8

Note from the Author

The events depicted in this book are related as I remember them. Others may have a different recollection. I did my best not to misrepresent anyone or any event in any way. I chose, in some cases, not to use individuals' full names to not call attention to them in any way they did not wish.

Dedication

I dedicate this book to Louise Lovdahl and Marvin Warter, both examples of educational excellence with a passion for young people.

To my godmother, Ms. Mary E. Pearson, who continues to teach me great life lessons and is the most dedicated and cool "godmom."

Table of Contents

Acknowledgments   ix

Foreword: Dr. Debbie Olufs   xiii

Introduction: Discovering
Servant Advocacy   xvii

1   Become a Servant Advocate   1

2   Expect an Outcome that Changes Lives   15

3   Take the Action Necessary to Make
        a Difference   29

4   Create Pivotal Moments that Redirect a
        Recipient's Journey   39

5   Only YOU can Choose to be a
        Change Agent   51

The Servant Advocate Challenge   65

The Underdog Must Become the Big Dog   69

Acknowledgments

I could not acknowledge anyone or anything without first acknowledging God, He who knew me in my mother's womb. He who knows every hair on my head. He who is the author and finisher of my faith. He who saw in me what no one else saw, knew or even believed. God, I thank you for every valley and mountain that you orchestrated in my life to get me to this place. Most of all, I thank you for being God.

To my two wonderful adult children, Je're Monet Harmon and Marlon Quincy Harmon, you are both the very best thing of mom and myself, and we are super proud of all you are and all you are becoming.

To my mother, Rose Mary Harmon, your sacrifice, commitment, and even your fifth-grade education was the spark that ignited me for more. Your struggle birthed my passion, and I am forever grateful for that. I love you, mother.

Thank you to my Big Momma, who allowed me to sit under her wing and just be. While others would say that I was spoiled, my big momma gave me all of the love and nurturing that my hands and heart could hold. She loved me to life and made sure I and those around me were aware of her love. Your unending love taught me what agape love truly was.

Thank you to my brothers, Vincent Borner, DeWayne Harmon, and my sister Shannon Harmon for loving me, being there for me, and pushing me to greatness even when you did not know that is what you were doing. I love you all and appreciate each of you.

To Louise Lovdahl and Marvin Warter, the love, nurturing, understanding, and caring that you both had for me was "priceless." You each made me better and encouraged me to dream beyond my situation or even what I could see. Your belief in me gave my dreams wings and purpose, and I cannot ever thank you enough for that. I only wish you were both still here today to see this moment when my story became a written piece that will hopefully transform someone else's life. You are truly missed but will never be forgotten.

Jim, Vicki, Carrie, and Chris Click, thank you for taking me in as a surrogate son and letting me see firsthand what happens when passion meets destiny. You all are exceptional individuals and an amazing family. Thank you all for your friendship and for loving me unconditionally.

Lastly, thank you to my Tucson church family. Thank you to my pastor, Dr. Amanda Goodson, her husband, Brother Lonnie Goodson, and my friend and spiritual father, Pastor Willie Coleman, and his wife, Leading Lady Shirley Coleman. You have each been pivotal in my life and my molding while on the potter's wheel. You prayed for me and with me, and you have offered counsel and an open ear. You have been my Hur and Aaron, holding me up when I got weak and tired. You never judged me but loved me unconditionally. You also gave me correction in love when needed, and for that, I will forever be grateful.

God bless everyone who has impacted my life from birth through now. Your words have pushed me and given me hopes, dreams, and the room needed to grow and mature. Because of each of you and, most importantly, God, we can triumph together!

Last and certainly not least, Dr. Yvette Rice has been a tremendous blessing to me during my book project. She embraced my ability to speak, write, and sometimes shed a few tears while supporting me with writing this most intimate work of my lifetime. She was pivotal for me in ultimately finishing my first book. I am grateful!

Foreword

To know Marlon is to touch love. He chooses to approach each day joyfully and with wonder and love. With his infectious laughter, engaging smile, and overwhelming warmth, Marlon is truly someone who can make any day better. Whether he is in a group of twenty or two hundred, Marlon is the magnet. In a store full of Christmas decorations, he is the one that lights up, beckoning you to join.

Being friends with Marlon has genuinely been one of my greatest gifts. His resilience in the face of daunting odds is extraordinary. Born into poverty and primarily raised by his great-grandmother, he did not know if heat or food would be available on any given day. Marlon started school in kindergarten and was immediately given extra help. Early on, school did not go well. Teacher turnover was a problem. As a third grader, he was paddled, and it was not until the end of the third grade when his mom insisted on a teacher change that he began to enjoy school. After repeating third grade, Marlon still struggled in reading but could finally experience regular math. He was in sixth grade before he had an African American teacher. In junior high, he continued to struggle academically and was primarily in basic classes. Generally, the help he received involved doing the work for him. In spite of this, in high school, Marlon became class president, ran the school store and was leader of Pledge–a group against alcohol and drug use.

Racism was prevalent in Marlon's hometown of Kenosha, Wisconsin, and played in the difficulties his teacher's experienced in having him assessed for learning disabilities. It was only during his senior year after a concerned teacher threatened legal action against the school district that he was assessed. Unfortunately, the support did not equate to teaching him to read or write but focused on doing work for him to get him through school.

Marlon's mentor called me at this time, stating, "When you meet Marlon, you will understand," and I did. A bright, industrious young man, in the middle of tenth grade, Marlon's GPA was 1.8. His reading comprehension skills were mid-fifth grade level, and writing was even lower. His language-based learning disability made it difficult for him to sound out and spell words, challenges which significantly impacted his overall literacy skills. In spite of that, working 4-5 hours out of class for every hour in class and taking advantage of virtually all available resources, he graduated not only from high school, but college as well. Writing a book when dyslexia is one of the most challenging undertakings one can experience, and Marlon did it fearlessly.

Resilience can be visualized as a sailboat on the ocean, where waves and currents are constantly influencing one's trajectory. For some, the slightest wave can take them off course or capsize them. Marlon was faced with tidal waves and managed to stay afloat, reach his goals, and thrive.

One of my favorite stories regarding Marlon happened just a few years ago. He had officiated at my son's wedding. During the reception, I saw Marlon and my nephew laughing hilariously at a table. My nephew was also dyslexic and combatting thoughts of whether or not he would be able to read books to his young daughters. He shared that he had read a story about the Nile Virus being found in a field near his daughters' daycare in a dead cow. He read the article over and over, knowing there were no cows near his daughters' school. On his sixth reading, he realized that he had read "crow" as "cow." Through this brief time of mentoring laughter,

Marlon was able to significantly alleviate my nephew's increasing parenting concerns.

As Archbishop Desmond Tutu stated, "Joy is much bigger than happiness. While happiness is often seen as being dependent on external circumstances, joy is not."[1] Although joy is elusive for most of us, most of the time, with Marlon, it appears to be his innate birthright. Most fortunately, he has the ability to multiply his joy through those he meets. Marlon is the rare individual that upon meeting him, leaves you better for the encounter. He is positive and moral and can teach others to find joy in spite of barriers. His gratitude for events and people nurtures wonder. He embodies the concept of being the change, which is inspirationally depicted in his book, *Triumphing in My Dyslexic World*. This book openly shares both his struggles and triumphs and describes how his mentors and his faith have helped him become the amazing man he is. The concept of paying it forward is fully embodied by Marlon through his book, and we are better because of this.

Deb Olufs
PhD in Special Education
Retired Educational Specialist

---

1   Dalai Lama, Desmond Tutu, and Douglas Carlton Abrams, *The Book of Joy: Lasting Happiness in a Changing World*. Avery Publishing Group. September 20, 2016

Introduction

Discovering Servant Advocacy

O h yes, you shaped me first inside, then out; you formed me in my mother's womb. I thank you, High God—you're breathtaking! Body and soul, I am marvelously made! I worship in adoration—what a creation! You know me inside and out, you know every bone in my body; You know exactly how I was made, bit by bit, how I was sculpted from nothing into something. Like an open book, you watched me grow from conception to birth; all the stages of my life were spread out before you, the days of my life all prepared before I'd even lived one day. (Psalms 139: 13 – 16)

As a man of faith, I believe that I am fearfully and wonderfully made. Yet, I questioned the afflictions of living with a learning disability at points in my life.

I have pondered what my life would have been like without underlying dyslexic reading abnormalities. For me, dyslexic abnormalities meant it was challenging to pronounce words from print and understandably read them. I was placed in small reading groups where I felt isolated because I could not keep up with the rest of my peers.

Going undiagnosed from kindergarten through the eleventh grade, my journey includes days of triumph and defeat. I did not attend pre-school. Thus, my kindergarten experience was shifted from a half-day to an all-day program because I needed additional assistance. By the time I reached the third grade, I was frustrated, developing disrespectful tendencies because I could not read and understand like my peers in the classroom. I didn't realize what I didn't know. In the eighth grade, I was referred for a learning disability assessment by a school advisor. Unfortunately, her request was overlooked, so I was passed along from one grade level to another with limited reading comprehension, although I could function verbally.

I have spotted memories, some good and some not so good, growing up as a kid in Kenosha, Wisconsin. I recall the time I witnessed my dad come into the house and fight with my mother. I ran into the kitchen, grabbed a fork from the drawer, and poked my dad with it while I screamed at him to stop scaring my mother. My mother was not formally educated, and she spent some of my younger years in a local work-release program. Raised in my first nine years by my maternal great-grandmother, known as "Big Mama," it's been said that I was a spoiled kid. My Big Mama's education level did not go beyond the third grade. Although she could read, my family did not stress the value of an education.

Since school was so hard for me, I often told Big Mama that I was sick, staying home from school multiple days at a time. Big Mama always believed me, so she would call the school and say that I would be out sick. As the absenteeism piled up, I continued to fall behind more and more. During elementary school, I had to always go to Title One and later Chapter One classes with two other classmates, Ann and Joe. I felt like we were the "three stooges."

The most painful time of my early years of learning happened on the last day of school, of the Third Grade. Even after 50 years later, I could still clearly recall how I felt, knowing that I was leaving Lincoln Elementary School for that summer as a third-grader, and I would have to return to school in the fall as a third-grader. I was despondent because I thought I would move along with all my friends. Miserably, I took the longest walk of my life from the school building to my house just down the street.

Upon arriving home, my brother Dewayne and some

neighborhood friends were standing outside of the Bedford family home directly across the road from our house. They were all chatting, laughing, and just having fun as they planned how they would spend the summer. As I got closer to the Bedford's house, they called me over to ask me about my grades. The most hurtful thing of my entire life, then and even now, was that my very own brother called me "flunky" after learning that I would be a third grader again. Dewayne's word, "flunky," wounded me more than my abduction and attempted molestation by a mentally ill neighbor in their family's garage when I was younger. Both experiences were painful. However, being called "flunky" by my brother while the other children listened made deep cuts in my psyche.

How does a young black man with learning disabilities, raised in a dysfunctional environment, grow up to lead, work, and compete in the marketplace as a successful adult? The answer is tied to the resolve in the innermost parts of my belly that told me, "I am marvelously made!" My story is one of hope and resilience while choosing not to allow the world to count me out. My definition of resilience is that I find my eyes open again after the last event or occurrence I did not think I could get through. Breath is still coming out of my nostrils, meaning I can forge ahead one more day. I encountered Servant Advocates that fought for me and pushed me to maximize my potential on my journey. Unfortunately, I also faced those who chose to do the work for me instead of preparing me to succeed from my own efforts.

Why share my story now? I believe it is essential that the inner "Servant Advocate" in everyone listens, acts, and be stirred up on behalf of the nearly seven million disabled students in the United States of America.[1] These numbers do not include the diagnosed and undiagnosed adults who face similar obstacles in this country daily. I am a Servant Advocate. My definition of Servant Advocate is the person who advocates for those who cannot fight or stand in the gap for themselves. These advocates place themselves in the shoes of those suffering from learning disabilities to feel what they feel and to hold up their arms when those who need assistance feel like giving up. If I share my story, I believe it will encourage parents, educators, clergy, and employers like you to get what I call "SOAPY." This acronym was inspired by my brother, Vincent Edward Borner.

Initially, I used the acronym "SOAPY" without considering the connotation of being soapy. The word soapy means to be lathered up or become foam-covered. Vincent reminded me that being a Servant Advocate meant there will be times when your hands get dirty (figuratively) through the difficulties of helping someone achieve beyond the challenges of dyslexia.

---

1   Katherine Schaeffer. "As schools shift to online learning amid pandemic, here's what we know about disabled students in the U.S.," Pew Research. https://www.pewresearch.org/fact-tank/2020/04/23/as-schools-shift-to-online-learning-amid-pandemic-heres-what-we-know-about-disabled-students-in-the-u-s/?amp=1. April 23, 2020.

S	Become a **Servant Advocate** for adults and children with learning disabilities.
O	Expect an **Outcome** that changes lives.
A	Take the **Action** necessary to make a difference in the lives of those who need you.
P	Create **Pivotal** moments that redirect the recipient's journey through the challenges faced.
Y	Only **You** can choose to be a change agent in the lives of others.

As you read about my story, I hope you are challenged to embrace the need. I also hope you recognize that somewhere out in the vast number of people you encounter daily, there is someone that needs a Servant Advocate. As you read my story, I pray that you will not stand on the sideline, but you will choose to get "SOAPY" like someone did for me.

1

Become a Servant Advocate

"⁣³⁴⁻³⁶ *Then the King will say to those on his right, 'Enter, you who are blessed by my Father! Take what's coming to you in this kingdom. It's been ready for you since the world's foundation. And here's why:*

I was hungry and you fed me,
I was thirsty, and you gave me a drink,
I was homeless and you gave me a room,
I was shivering and you gave me clothes,
I was sick and you stopped to visit,
I was in prison and you came to me.'

³⁷⁻⁴⁰ *"Then those 'sheep' are going to say, 'Master, what are you talking about? When did we ever see you hungry and*

feed you, thirsty and give you a drink? And when did we ever see you sick or in prison and come to you?' Then the King will say, 'I'm telling the solemn truth: Whenever you did one of these things to someone overlooked or ignored, that was me—you did it to me." (Matthew 25: 34–40)

Some may ask, "are you angry with your brother?" My answer is "No." I love my brother. Through that experience, Dewayne helped me become who I am today. I allow that day to propel me even now. Yes, the third-grade repeat year was painful, but it was the turning point of my life. God took that severe pain and turned it into an incredible, life-changing opportunity.

Over that year, the nurturing and encouragement that I received from my first Servant Advocate Encounter broke that barrier or wall of frustration that surrounded me. Some actions of Servant Advocates are done instinctively because that is who they are. These advocates serve others intentionally without personal motives attached to their cause. They assist humanity naturally with the thought that everyone deserves an opportunity to fulfill their God-given purpose. Servant Advocates may not know what that person's final story looks like, but they want to be a part of the process.

During the behavior crisis I was experiencing while repeating the third grade, I befriended Pat Ennis. Pat's parents were active in Boys Scouts. His mother, Dorothy, was a Webelos Den Mother and a Cub Scout helper, and his father, Bill, was a Scout Leader. Moving beyond the racial divides in 1980, Pat and I became best friends. As of the publishing of this book, we are still brothers from a different mother.

Pat's dad took me under his wings, and I attended camping trips with their family. I went religiously on their summer vacations. I learned to canoe in the lake and experience nature in ways I would have never imagined as a little boy. Bill gave his heart in teaching me how to fish, literally, how to carve my derby car from wood, and how to tie all my essential knots to earn my badges. His passion for making me a part of their family exposed me to things a young African American child with my background may have never experienced.

In my grandmother's day, she would have said I went across the tracks. However, it was known as "across the park" in Kenosha. Lincoln Park served as the dividing line of the races, the same as "across the tracks" is known in Mississippi. Yet, I traveled across Lincoln Park almost every day to hang out with Pat and his family, as well as other students and their families that embraced me. These parents became Servant Advocates for me. They knew there was something different about Marlon beyond my race. Still, they never allowed those unique characteristics to hinder their desires to help me.

I became a member of the Cub Scouts and quickly

moved up to the Webelo Scouts. The experience of moving up was frightening for me because I was a year older than Pat and the other guys. To move up to the Webelos meant I would have to make a bold step and go to a different community of boys I did not know. Nor did they know about my learning disabilities. Bill encouraged me and told me I could successfully take that step. I did, and a year later, Pat and the others joined me. *The boys were back together again.*

Bill's job as a traveling engineer took him away from his role as a Scout Master for multiple years. The guys and I ended up with Wally Myers and Joe Dalton as our Scout Master and Assistant Scout Master. I entrenched myself in scouting and increased my leadership responsibility for my troop while advancing my rank. Although Bill was no longer in a leadership role, he actively participated when he could. At 12 years old, I wrote Bill a note promising in poorly written grammar, "I will work to become an Eagle Scout."

On the night I was awarded my Eagle Scout badge my senior year of high school, Bill presented me that note in a glass frame and said, "You earned this back." Bill kept that note all those years, and he continued to be an advocate in my life. I still have that framed note to this day.

Looking back, if I had not repeated the third grade, Pat and I would not have become friends. I believe, according to the Bible, "...all that happens to us is working for

our good if we love God and are fitting into his plans."
(Romans 8:28 TLB) I know God intervened in my life.

————

Outside of scouting, I encountered my first black teacher,
Henry Thurman, another Servant Advocate. Henry introduced me to the world of sign language. He was a Special
Olympics basketball coach, and he allowed me to coach
and travel with him and the team. He also took me out
of my community and exposed me to other opportunities for growth. My tender heart for others in need grew
during this time because of Henry's empathy towards
me. Having that heart of compassion and empathy is a
required characteristic of a Servant Advocate. At the time
of this publishing, Henry and I remain in contact.

As one of Henry's pupils, I discovered a difference
between instructors. Some teachers gave me my schoolwork back marked with red and green ink. Those like
Henry called me to their desk and asked me what my
thoughts were. The more responsive teacher allowed me
to respond audibly.

A key to servant advocacy is not about always giving
someone what we think they need. It is more about
pulling the best out of that person in need through
coaching and nurturing. Henry used coachable moments
to pull out the knowledge inside me.

My high school mentor and advocate was Marvin N.

Warter (Marv). In 1988, I had a local Scout Master call me and ask if I was interested in meeting an instructor from the University of Wisconsin-Parkside regarding a possible scholarship opportunity. The fascinating thing is that Marv called the Scout Master about one of his other Eagle Scouts, Curtis Meeks. Curtis was another young African American and personal friend of mine. The Scout Master recognized it was not Curtis Meeks, the car junkie and young mechanic that would be interested in that possible opportunity, so he recommended me.

Marv and his wife, Shirley, were both schoolteachers who took me in and introduced me to philosophy, Socrates, and Plato. They exposed me to great books and talked to me about the Bible. Marv taught me the meaning of "Teach us to number our days, that we may gain a heart of wisdom." (Psalm 90:12 NIV). Through the Warters, I caught the meaning of that scripture because it was not taught with such understanding in my community church. Marv always said, "The best things in life are caught, not taught."

Marv also said, "live in an hour as a grain of sand, like today is your last day – live it to the fullest." In my community, we lived wondering how we would get our next meal. Yet, the Warters opened my mind and imagination with trips like seeing Madama Butterfly at the Lyric Opera House in Chicago, Illinois. Those types of exposures also changed the trajectory of my life. The

Warters' impact on my life was so broad I could never express it all in the pages of this book.

Although I had access to Earl Harmon, the man I knew to be my father, our relationship was not defined. At the time of the fork incident, he lived with another woman and her family in my community. At the age of five, another man, George Brown, told me he was my father, adding more confusion in my life. George was in a relationship with my mother at that time. Although I did not accept him as my father, we had a distant relationship until his passing in my adulthood. However, my surrogate fathers were Bill Ennis, Henry Thurman, and Marvin Warter. Their deeds towards me earned the right of fatherhood over my life more than any of those other men who said they were my father.

After the age of nine, I went from living totally with my great-grandmother to living with my siblings at my mother's house near my grandmother and great-grandmother's homes. However, I still spent time with my grandmother and great-grandmother every day.

My mother had "rent parties" to cover the cost of the rent. People paid to come to our house and party in our basement. My mother cooked hotdogs on the stove, and my brother was the DJ in the basement where they danced. I suppose we were early entrepreneurs unaware. Those rent parties were my mother's means of existence.

During the 1980s, my mom worked for the American Motors Corporation. However, she experienced multiple layoffs. Those layoffs had an impact on our economic situation. To compensate, my mother worked as a bartender, which is sometimes how we had food. A safe place was created for me when the Ennis family invited me to their home for a sleepover or Henry Thurman took me to a basketball game. I believe these advocates knew and felt like, "we might not be able to save all of them, but Marlon is worth the effort." However, I don't think they realized the shelter they created for my life at that time.

Because of the various outside connections with those who advocated for me, my sister, Shannon Harmon, and her best girlfriend, Shirley Moore, gave me the nickname "APK," referencing the character Alex P. Keaton from the sitcom *Family Ties*.[1] Shannon and Shirley's thoughts were that I was a "nerdy business type kid."

My mom struggled with depression. As children, we didn't know which mother would be home when we arrived. There were days when my siblings and I came home and found the blinds and curtains closed. The outlets provided by my grandmother and great grandmother, in addition to my siblings Dewayne and

[1]Gary David Goldberg, Lloyd Garver, & Alan Uger (Executive producers. *Family Ties* [Television series]. [With Michael J. Fox, Meredith Baxter, Michael Gross, Justin Bateman, Tina Yothers, & Brian Bonsall]. New York, NY: National Broadcasting Company. 1982.

Shannon, who sometimes lived with our dad, also created safe havens for us.

My mom's behavior was not intentional. It was her hard life of being a sixteen-year-old girl from Mississippi coming to Wisconsin to babysit her cousins to escape a brutal life of picking cotton in the south that contributed to her behavior. The move did not afford my mom the opportunities she desired. She started working a factory job which led to the men and drinking. My resolve in that situation was that my mother did the best she could with what she had.

At the age of 24, when mom introduced me to another man and told me he was my father, angrily, I decided I was too old to have another dad enter my life. Yet, through all this, I continue to love my mom and plan to help take care of her for the rest of her life. My motto is, "if I have it, she has it."

———

One of my most special female Servant Advocates was Louise Lovdahl. She came into my life at age 14. Louise was my Junior High School Music and Study Hall teacher, who later became my "I Took the Pledge" Advisor. The pledge was an afterschool club. A group of courageous junior high and later high school students decided to take a public stance that we would not use drugs or alcohol while still in school and under 18 years old. Additionally, we all pledged to leave a party or gathering that our peers hosted if they were drinking and smoking.

Both Ms. Lovdahl and Mrs. Deborah Filippelli, who worked at a different school, combined the two groups through their friendship and love for kids. Our pledge group became famous around Wisconsin and in Illinois. This was all during the Nancy Regan era of her "Just Say No" program. We became so renowned that our group filmed a video with the Chicago Bears.... They had the Super Bowl Shuffle, and we had the Pledger Shuffle. I recall us participating in a Chicago Parade alongside the Chicago Bears Team.

Louise Lovdahl became a surrogate mother for me. When she found me, she offered tough but encouraging love towards me. She challenged me to recite and practice my words audibly until I could accomplish it instead of doing everything for me. It wasn't punitive. She believed in my capabilities. I could not see those abilities at that moment, but they were later drawn out. Her advocacy taught me not to be afraid to speak during sizable public events.

Louise stood in the gap for me as a person and not just because of the circumstances. She made it known to those around her who I was in her life. Once, Louise won a contest to have the famous pencil artist, George Pollard, draw her picture. But, instead, she insisted I go to the sitting, stating, "Marlon, when you become famous, I want to be able to have your picture already in hand."

Louise's family accepted the relationship we had, even beyond the diversities of race and socioeconomic backgrounds. I believe the nurturing love she shared toward me put a hedge around me and pushed aside any negativity that might have existed amongst her family members. They respected me as a human, not as this black kid that needed special help.

Louise passed away in 2017. Several months before her death, she called me. Louise explained that she was dying due to an illness, and there were some things she wanted me to know, including that she loved me as though she had birthed me. Louise shared that she was planning her services in her garden, the most treasured place she had on this earth, and that she wanted me and my wife, Lisa, to come. Louise further shared that I had to be there because she wanted me to have that picture of me. Louise had saved that picture all these years. She arranged for us to attend the celebration of her beautiful life.

I showcase that cherished artistic sketch and the memorial card from Louise's services in my home office. I am constantly reminded that Louise gave everything she could, relative to me developing into the man she believed I would become. She had a great love for women and children, and their causes were her life's work and mission.

Maybe Louise's passion originated from the fact that she was adopted. Fortunately, she did have the opportunity to meet her birth mother. I also had that pleasure because, as a surrogate son, Louise allowed me into her personal world. At her funeral service, Louise's nephew, Myron, shared that he knew how much his aunt adored me.

———

Maybe their faith caused these Servant Advocates to operate from a different perspective relative to my life. Bill Ennis, Marvin Warter, Henry Thurman, and Louise Lovdahl's cornerstone was patience because they never gave up on me. I realize now that another one of the characteristics of a true Servant Advocate is patience,

Servant Advocates never give up on those they are chosen to serve. They are likened to Christ. When we do the most heinous thing, there is nowhere in the Bible I can find that the love of Christ Jesus is averse to the person becoming an overcomer. A Servant Advocate believes so profoundly inside that they will see a favorable result, that they actually "will out" the best for those being served.

Similarly, in the movie "Just Wright," the basketball player, Scott McKnight, played by actor Common, spoke of his physical therapist, Leslie Wright, played by Queen Latifah, saying, "She saw something in me that I didn't even see in myself. She believed in me so much, she practically willed me back to the game.[2]" My Servant Advocates willed

---

[2]Queen Latifah, Shakim Compere, & Debra Martin Chase (Producers), & Sanaa Hamri (Director). *Just Wright* [Motion picture]. [Written by Michael Elliott]. [With Queen Latifah, Common, & Paula Patton]. United States: Flavor Unit Entertainment. 2010.

me into the person I am today through their unwavering faith, believing that I am fearfully and wonderfully made.

My Scout Master, Bill Ennis, my teachers, Henry Thurman and Louise Lovdahl, Marvin Warter, and other people in my community helped me believe that I could do great things. Thankfully, these Servant Advocates operated from a higher place. Their intentions were to pull that "Marvelously Made Marlon" out of those challenging situations.

Retrospectively, I realize the call on my life to become a Servant Advocate was shaped by those who served me through my journey. Whether in the workplace, community, serving as a tutor, or in a church congregation, I choose to accept the Servant Advocate call. It is astonishing to see that even though I struggle with Dyslexia, I can still help others with similar problems.

Cub Scouts Pack 505 – 1979:
Marlon Harmon – Centered

2

Expect an Outcome that Changes Lives

"For I know the plans I have for you, declares the Lord, plans to prosper you and not to harm you, plans to give you hope and a future." (Jeremiah 29:11 NIV)

Becoming a Servant Advocate for people with learning disabilities is a genuine reward when the advocate witnesses change in the lives of those served. For example, one of the students I tutored now performs in Milwaukee in various crisis scenes at hospitals by playing the violin with his ensemble. He helps to bring healing to hurting people with his gifts and abilities. This same student served as a town council member and assisted with writing county legislation. These successful outcomes brought me great joy, fulfilling an expectation that I could make a difference in someone's life if I pursued Servant Advocacy.

My Scout Master, Bill Ennis, kept that poorly written promise of becoming an Eagle Scott because he expected a life-changing outcome for me. When I met Bill, my focus was not aligned toward scouting. My background did not include understanding how becoming a scout could change my life. Bill's intervention in my life caused a realignment toward purposeful activities to help me succeed. I went from small-town thinking to understanding life from a worldview. For me, these new experiences realigned the thoughts, "I can't" to "I can, and I will."

I never considered attending college before my experiences as an Eagle Scout. I dared to dream because of Bill's expectations for a hope and a future for my life. Unfortunately, not everyone around me saw my ability to dream as positive. After my father, Earl Harmon, remarried, his new mother-in-law sarcastically referred to me as a "dreamer." Yet, God transformed those condescending overtones meant to discourage me into a means that pushed me to my new reality.

In Genesis 37:5 (NIV), when Joseph shared his dreams with his brothers, "they hated him all the more." I do not believe my father's mother-in-law hated me, but it made me aware that not every person around me was an advocate for me. However, I did not allow those words she spoke to define me. A Servant Advocate must understand that sometimes the words they speak to their mentee will be battling counterproductive negativity when that mentee is in their main environment. Like my experiences, some mentees will also face hills and valleys in their quest as they move beyond their current state of being. Many of them seek to overcome adverse circumstances. As a Servant Advocate, anticipate your mentee will encounter a realignment of their perspectives related to their abilities to achieve far beyond their original starting point or expectations. I believe Louise Lovdahl insisted I have my portrait sketched by George Pollard because she hoped for a positive realignment of my life. After all, she advocated on my behalf.

As a Servant Advocate, your expectations for your mentee should be high. However, as the advocate, you will also face humbling experiences. You will encounter hills and valleys like your mentee while working with them because it takes time for the mentee to live through their overcoming moments. The pace of growth depends on the mentee, and for those developing times, you can only help or go as far as the mentee will allow for any given day. Your mentee must be allowed to develop organically in a non-threatening posture. This may result in you feeling like they are moving backward at times instead of moving forward. However, there are emotions that your mentee must conquer along with any educational development. The stench of those emotional changes can also be sobering.

I experienced one of those emotional moments in the assembly hall of Lincoln Junior High School in Kenosha. I was rehearsing a speech because I was one of the representatives for the "I Took the Pledge" Program Louise and Debbie spearheaded. Louise Lovdahl and Deborah Filippelli were known for their standards of excellence in every project they pursued. Louise was adamant about my articulation and ownership of the words in the speech because she knew I could represent our organization well when we visited other schools and groups. I remember Louise saying to me, "Marlon, you get over there in that corner, and you just, read it, read it, read it." I shrugged my shoulders and headed toward the corner, mumbling words that I knew I was not adult enough to say. At that moment, I became overwhelmed because I did not understand why Louise was so stern with me. It was not until after I successfully presented during an assembly that I comprehended why she was so persistent.

Louise had expectations of me living a disciplined life because she wanted the world to see the best "Marlon Harmon" possible. She believed that "just enough to get by" was not suited for the future God had for my life (Jerimiah 29:11). Louise's level of expectation for me to be more disciplined eventually reaped a harvest. Through hindsight, I now know that if I had not relentlessly practiced and persisted, I would continue to fall short for the remainder of my life. That memory of those words, "read it, read it, read it," are forever etched in my mind because it was another turning point that produced a life-changing result through one of my Servant Advocates. As an adult professional, I regularly stand in front of audiences as a presenter and trainer. Additionally, I have served as a minister for more than 14 years, weekly preaching and teaching the Word of God and praying for those in need.

Louise gave me a new sense of the word "drive" that continues to evolve even in adulthood. Nearing 50 years old, my brother, Vincent, and I took a 75-mile bike ride. As it got hotter on the journey, it became more challenging. Even though the headwinds were coming toward us, I knew we had to get back by a specific time because of other obligations. The understanding of drive that Louise imprinted in my brain rose to the occasion.

My interpretation of the word "drive" is the point where everything I have inside me is exhausted, and all I have left is vision. I did not have any physical energy left inside me on that bike trip. But I had a vision of us getting back to the car on time. When we reached the last bike stop that was five miles from my vehicle, I realized that Louise's sternness from those days at Lincoln produced a never-ending outcome.

Expected outcomes may lead to unexpected events that seem like setbacks. Consequently, the Servant Advocate must operate in a place of faith, believing that there will be a breakthrough at some point. Because some days it will look like change is not possible. There are times you, the Servant Advocate, will vicariously live through the pain of their mentee. While serving me in the neighborhood where I lived, Marv had flashbacks of his life. Even though the community was different from his childhood experiences, there were some similarities. However, the area's culture had changed, providing minimal access to opportunities for development. Acknowledging those differences and the enormous amount of lack was humbling for Marv.

Marv and the other Servant Advocates shared their resources freely because of these eye-opening experiences. Fortunately for me, Louise Lovdahl became so frustrated at one point in her quest to get me assistance she threatened that my mother would file a lawsuit against the school system.

I was struggling tremendously with my schoolwork in the ninth grade. Louise requested I be tested. Her request was overlooked by all responsible parties, including the principal and vice-principal. At this point, I was no longer that angry child from the third grade. Instead, I was known to many as mild-mannered. This "new" calmer Marlon was not considered a critical case that

warranted immediate action, such as placing me in reme-
dial classes. My Math and English grades continued to
fall, but the school system continued to pass me along. I
felt like I was just there in this nonexistent state of being.

Finally, out of frustration, Louise invoked my mother's name regarding a lawsuit without her knowledge to
get the administrators to provide me with the attention I
needed and deserved. Immediately, the school psychologist intervened. Even though it was a sputtering startup,
Louise's tantrum got the process for help started. By the
time I reached the twelfth grade, the much-needed diagnosis process to determine the type of learning disability
I had moved faster.

There is no room for arrogance as a Servant Advocate.
The opportunity to advocate for these positive outcomes
is also a type of "on-the-job training" for advocates. Each
mentee is uniquely created, and their experiences of
change are also unique. These are not "one size fits all"
scenarios. Thus, being a Servant Advocate requires an agile
demeanor with flexibility for growth and a mindset pep-
pered with faith.

Henry Thurman knew my case was not a "one size fits
all" situation. He was one of the first black male career
professionals that spent valuable time with me. Henry
used those opportunities to assist him with Special
Olympics Basketball to build a unique relationship as
a Servant Advocate. His demeanor was tough enough

to keep the reigns on me to prevent me from getting in trouble. But it was loving enough to remind me that I could achieve greatness as a young black man from Kenosha, Wisconsin. Henry's influence was far-reaching in my family. He introduced me and my brother Vincent to the world of tennis. Vincent's son, Braxton, is now a professional tennis instructor.

Servant advocacy includes increased curiosity for both the mentee and the advocate to pursue a positive expected outcome. As a Servant Advocate, you must internally interview your mentee because you only have surface knowledge about them at the beginning of the relationship. The inner makeup and thoughts of your mentee are unknown to you. You must determine the bandwidth of that mentee to understand your limits relative to how deep they will allow you to investigate their struggles and mindset; and find out their mental toughness. Therefore, you, the advocate, must learn to ask questions along the journey to really get to know your mentee.

Marv taught me how to get to know someone, and I believe what he shared with me is universal. He said to "listen to what that person says about themselves, watch what that person does during an encounter, and listen to what other people are saying about that person." Listen to what your mentee is saying about themselves. Study your mentee's actions when you are around them. Listen carefully to what others are saying about your mentee.

Your mentee is interviewing you as well. Somewhere along the journey, there will be a peaked interest for both of you. That peak occurred between Bill Ennis and me when scouting became our common ground. I wanted to become a Cub and Webelo Scout. However, Bill and the other Scout Leaders did not see this interest as an ordinary opportunity to sign up another young man. They saw my peaked interest as an investment and a chance for a breakthrough that could lead to an expected outcome. Bill encouraged me to come over to the other side of Lincoln Park to enter the world of scouting. During those interactions, these scout leaders were watching. They listened and used those times to increase their knowledge base about my capabilities and limitations. They looked for ways they could help me develop to my maximum potential.

I call these encounters the "scoop and sift" process commonly referred to as Placer Mining used by gold miners back in the days of the California Gold Rushes. Every time there is an opportunity to interview your mentee through peak encounters, you pan to see what is there. Patience is required because there may only be a small nugget that is valuable to the learning process in a large batch of substances. There will be other times you sift, and there isn't anything to claim. But the intrinsic desire to see your mentee advance will keep you returning for more opportunities to find gold and precious stones that produce positive outcomes in their lives.

A Servant Advocate must also realize other miners are working to strike gold. My journey involved multiple advocates working on my behalf at various points in my life. I am reminded of a biblical passage of scripture where the Apostle Paul shares the process of an individual's introduction to the Lord. It says, "[5] What, after all is Apollo? And what is Paul? Only servants, through whom you came to believe —as the Lord has assigned to each his task. [6] I planted the seed, Apollos watered it, but God has been making it grow. [7] So neither the one who plants nor the one who waters is anything, but only God, who makes things grow." (1 Corinthians 3: 5 – 7 NIV)

Each part played by the different Servant Advocates is significant in the mentee's outcome. However, the significance of those encounters may not be known until later.

———

Servant Advocates must be sophisticated enough to know there is a balance. However, that balance may not always feel good. Meaning, as Servant Advocates, there are times when we must release and let go because our mentee has matured to a different place in their lives and moved on. For example, when it was time for me to marry and move on, Louise Lovdahl understood her advocating time was served. She saw me reach adulthood, graduate from college, and get married. Although she did not witness everything God is doing in my life, I believed she died in faith, knowing that God would complete the work he had begun in me. Now, the things I accomplish, I do in her memory.

As a Servant Advocate, you must dare to go places other people would not go to see your mentee succeed. You and your mentee must demonstrate a readiness to explore and strategize. In some cases, the mentee has been overlooked and left with little hope for outcomes that produce a fruitful life because others could not see their value. However, you must recognize that mentee is your assignment for legacy to occur, and that person's life is valuable. Initially, the mentee may be timid because of their past experiences. But you as the Servant Advocate must be postured to anticipate one step, one circumstance at a time to focus on to achieve a life-changing outcome. There will be times when you, the advocate, embrace the pains and aggravations of your mentee as though they were your own.

My Psychology professor, Dr. Larry Hamilton from Carthage College, sat me down at the college and told me, "I know you understand what is happening." "However, for whatever reason, you are not able to demonstrate it on an exam." "I know by our conversations; you know what is going on." Dr. Hamilton then said, "Quite frankly, you are perplexing to me. But I am not done because even though it doesn't come out on your examinations, there is no way we can have these dialogs, and you can participate in this classroom if you didn't have the knowledge and understanding of the content." "I say this because you can stand toe to toe with your peers." Dr. Hamilton's "out of the box" thinking made him a risk-taker. It took his mental drive as my advocate to be willing to take that last shot on my behalf and push me forward.

The journey to experiencing expected outcomes for some mentees will take longer than their Servant Advocate anticipates. For example, initially reaching the Promise Land was an eleven-day journey for the Israelites. Yet, it took them 40 years because of their lack of trust and buy-in with the Lord. Likewise, God did not reveal the expected days of my journey in advance. Yet, the Servant Advocates surrounding me remained constant in their faith, seeking an outcome that could change my life forever.

Through the process of this journey, both the mentee and the Servant Advocate are liberated. Their conversations are now open and candid because topics relating to the pains and frustrations of learning to communicate, whether orally or written, are discussed without hesitancy.

I did experience positive expected outcomes. Through the years of my journey, I began to openly talk to my Servant Advocates. They knew they could candidly express themselves regarding my excursion. With a copy of this book in my hand, I plan to sit down with those surviving advocates who helped me and let them know how much they liberated me. I can now share my testimony freely. I want them to know that the times they invested in me were well served, and their legacy will continue through me as a Servant Advocate.

I see their legacy when I mentor and encourage my own children, Je're and Quincy, as well as those strangers God places in my path. I desire to influence positive outcomes in the lives of others who need a Servant Advocate.

3

Take the Action Necessary to Make a Difference

What good is it, my brothers and sisters, if someone claims to have faith but has no deeds? Can such faith save them? Suppose a brother or a sister is without clothes and daily food. If one of you says to them, "Go in peace; keep warm and well fed," but does nothing about their physical needs, what good is it? ... (James 2:14 – 26 NIV)

*A*re you ready to rise up into action with a leap of faith? Before you answer, let me share what "taking action" did for me. When I think of Henry Thurman, his action allowed me to leap into his world and come along with him on his life's journey. Marv Warter saw my story in the newspaper. As a Servant Advocate, he sprang into action by immediately making phone calls on my behalf. Louise Lovdahl's actions included not allowing me to settle but pushing me into the realization that I could learn to read and speak publicly. It was more about taking that first step with me than having all the correct answers with each of them.

For me, an action meant trusting those people who took a leap of faith on my behalf. I didn't know them, but I felt they wanted to make a difference in my life. I took that first step of faith with Bill Ennis to become a scout. I took another step by signing up for the pledge program through Louise and learning how to speak to the masses. These steps took courage and faith. Even with the uncertainties I felt, I moved forward.

Marv used the act of walking as an example for me. He said, "walking is leaning forward and preventing yourself from falling. It's an action." Walking is all about moving one foot after the other. The journey of getting *SOAPY* requires movement. It requires all of us to LEAP. "What does LEAP mean," one might ask? Reflecting on my story, it means:

L – Leading the way forward by taking that first step.

E – Exercising your faith, putting your doubts of failure aside.

A – Acting as though someone's life depends on your steps forward; it does!

P – Persevering even when the world says, "It won't work."

Even though the mentee and the Servant Advocate must act, the LEAP process is twofold. For the mentee, the LEAP process embodies mentally and emotionally moving beyond all obstacles that stand between them and unlimited opportunities. For the Servant Advocate, the LEAP process involves opening closed doors that limit opportunities for their mentee. For every obstacle the mentee faces, the advocate must seek ways to work through or around that present situation to open another door.

The way forward for me in the third grade was an eye-opener. The visual of seeing things like the stress-free life of Pat Ennis was something that I did not have privy to on the other side of Lincoln Park. On Pat's side of the park, there appeared to be a sense of abundance. While on my side of the park, I dealt with the hustle and bustle of trying to be a family, wondering where our next meal would come from. My analogy would be that even though there wasn't complete lack, our "barnyard was not fully stocked."

There was also a sense of calmness in the Ennis' household. Our family had faith that we would make it through. But to move beyond the belief of "having just enough to having plenty" was not something my family could ascertain at the time. Even though there were differences in our households, including race, Pat and I shared that sense of calmness because we were just innocent kids that wanted to play together. Fortunately, our parents looked beyond the differences between the two families and allowed us to play.

Relative to the LEAP process, Bill Ennis took the lead on the way forward for my life. He used scouting as an engagement tool to create movement. Pat and I had already established a trusting relationship in the safety of the playground and the classroom at Lincoln Elementary School. We had our teachers' security, which let us know it was okay to be friends and bond even though we came from two very different worlds. Thus, I felt secure enough to participate in scouting through Bill's invite.

My mother did not take me to the scout meetings; I went independently. Yet, I felt at ease because of my friendship with Pat and knowing that he would also be attending the meetings. My peers and the scout leaders, Pat's parents, welcomed me. I also felt welcomed at Pat's home because of his family's open arms. The same love and warmth I experienced in scouting I received in their home.

Ironically, the elementary and junior high school that I attended was named after President Lincoln, the person responsible for the Emancipation Proclamation.

Additionally, the landmark that separated our neighborhoods was Lincoln Park. In these school facilities, I began the steps to receive my personal emancipation from the bondage of an undiagnosed dyslexic world through the faith of those Servant Advocates who fought for a new life for me.

My steps of faith led me to discovery. One of those first opportunities for discovery was participating in the scout's Wood Derby held in the Lincoln Elementary Gym. My scout leaders created comradery around carving, building, and painting a piece of wood that was transformed into a car. Making that car from a woodblock and then racing it was a movement of accomplishment for me.

Similarly, people like Bill Ennis, who chose to become my Servant Advocate, took me, a chunk of pinewood, and carved, shaped, and molded me into who I have become. They exercised their faith to believe there was more to Marlon Harmon than what appeared on the surface. Every time Bill had the opportunity to engage with me collectively with the other scouts and individually, I was challenged to make decisions that brought maturity and a more significant commitment to seek higher achievements.

When I think of persevering even when the world says, "It won't work," I reflect on Henry Thurman's actions as a Servant Advocate. I began to have behavioral and academic breakthroughs in the third and fourth grades. As a repeat third-grader and fourth-grader, my grades improved to Cs in math, science, and social studies. However, I encountered a setback in the fifth grade. Although my grades improved in other subjects, I continued to trail behind my peers in reading and writing. My fifth-grade teacher used mostly worksheets and workbooks educationally, which was less supportive of my academic needs. This teaching style sent me spiraling into a decline attitudinally and academically. I sought to move beyond the disciplinary boundaries this teacher established to the point of defiance in some cases. Thus, by the time I entered Henry's sixth-grade class, I was seen by him as a misguided young man who needed significant mentoring.

Since I repeated the third grade, I was physically more mature than other students in my class. At that time, the transition from elementary to junior high school occurred after the sixth grade, leaving me the oldest of my classmates. Henry sensed that I was trying to deal with that age gap emotionally, creating a stronger mentorship bond. Whenever I got into behavioral trouble, Henry was there mediating.

During one of those times I misbehaved, Henry scolded me profusely because I made an inappropriate gesture towards one of my female classmates. I now realize that Henry knew my actions could have been detrimental to my future. He did not want to see me become another statistic from a young misguided black male perspective. I can still remember those scourging words, "Boy, what are you doing?" as though it was a recent occurrence. Henry made me apologize to the young lady. Thus, my conduct went from being a practical joker to becoming the center stage of a disciplinary action.

Fortunately for me, I did not perceive Henry's actions as an attack on me or my character, but as someone who knew he needed to intervene to save my life and help me mature. Henry demonstrated a sternness I had never experienced before by a male figure. Yet, it was deserving. For the first time in my life, I received discipline from a personal "father figure." I never behaved that way during scouting, so Bill never needed to discipline me. The behavioral problems I indulged in were usually in the school environment.

Henry's mentorship activity led to increased responsibilities for me at school. I became a crossing guard. I also started attending sign language training events and working with the Special Olympics during that time. These additional responsibilities created upward movement in my life and our relationship as mentor and mentee. Even though I eventually moved on to Lincoln Junior High School, I continued visiting Henry. Using my story to inspire others, Henry's Servant Advocacy expanded beyond "Marlon Harmon," the young man he handed a lifeline. Unfortunately for me, the dyslexia I faced every day still had not been adequately diagnosed. The lack of diagnosis meant I still had to persevere without knowing why I was struggling to read and write at the level of my peers. However, Henry and Bill Ennis still opened a platform for me to share my story and breakthroughs, which caused me to gain a level of respect from my peers and some of the other teachers in my school. I even received the "Most Improved" and "Citizenship" awards in school that year. My attitude towards academics began to change for the better.

I understood that I was not alone, which boosted me to move forward with courage. Through the LEAP process with Henry and Bill, I even began to move beyond the third-grade incident with my brother. I saw myself as no longer being that "flunky" who was mocked in my neighbor's front yard. I was now Marlon, and I could see someone who could LEAP into action even in my own eyes.

———

Like me, there may be a time in your life when you feel like something crushed you, or the weight seems so heavy that you feel like you cannot overcome it. Then, along comes at least one Servant Advocate that is willing to LEAP for you. Be ready to take that LEAP with them in faith to move your life forward. Or you may be that

Servant Advocate whose time has come to LEAP on behalf of someone you know.

The LEAP process is not isolated to a wounded child facing developmental hardships. Servant Advocates are needed throughout the workforce. In multiple industries, an adult with many gifts and abilities is being held back because someone was afraid to LEAP with them into a new life of possibilities. I believe every real leader has or will have an opportunity to become a Servant Advocate if they are willing. These opportunities can help a person create movement in their lives, inspiring their faith to excel beyond the limits the world has placed upon them. This opportunity may or may not be related to dyslexia. Yet, the spirit of advocacy is crying out for someone in need.

For example, my Commercial Driver's License (CDL) instructor is one I can say created additional movement in my advancement to overcome another barrier. This trainer was very patient with me, and he was also encouraging. I was learning to drive a semi-truck, which was not easy for me. The most challenging part of learning to navigate the semi was backing up. I remember my instructor saying to me one day in a kind and joking fashion, "You will eventually get it. I just hope I am not retired by the time you do." The instructor knew there was potential even though I struggled to accomplish my goal of receiving my CDL license. Although it was short-lived, that CDL instructor took a LEAP on my behalf for that moment in time.

In every aspect of our lives as dyslexics, "the struggle is real," whether to learn to read or write, work on a job, attend college, or get a driver's license. The key is having someone willing to become that advocate to help you succeed. In this instance, the driving instructor leaped with me. I received my CDL license and drove a semi-truck at one point in my career.

4

Create Pivotal Moments that Redirect a Recipient's Journey

"See, I am doing a new thing! Now it springs up; do you not perceive it? I am making a way in the wilderness and streams in the wasteland." (Isaiah 43:19 NIV)

When I think of pivotal moments in my life, one of the first persons I think of is Dr. Debbie Olufs. Debbie understood that Servant Advocacy is not an occasion to feel sorry for someone but an opportunity to redirect a recipient's journey in ways that unlocks destiny and purpose.

One of the most pivotal breakthroughs of my dyslexic

diagnosis came through Debbie when I was entering my senior year at George Nelson Tremper High School. At the time, Debbie was a diagnostician, specifically working with students like me. She worked outside of the school district and was finally able to provide additional testing and a specific diagnosis for my case. There were many unknowns relative to my academic ability until that time. I was constantly asking myself, "Why am I struggling? Why am I always behind? Why can't I understand things like my peers?" Yet, there were other areas of my life where I was strong and astute, demonstrating a higher intellect.

Like the two other students who faced the same challenges relative to reading, I was intelligent enough to know something was wrong and that we were removed from the regular classroom because the teachers saw us as "special." But not "special" in what our peers considered a positive way.

While my ability to comprehend as I read was subpar, I did manage to do well in history because of the oral requirements during class. These types of classes became my "fall to" because I could produce in those environments. They gave me hope and an opportunity to pivot in a positive direction.

Debbie understood the power of a pivotal moment. She became a Servant Advocate who worked with me during high school. Debbie later shadowed me during my college journey as she worked on her dissertation at the University of Illinois. Debbie eventually invited me to come to Chicago and speak to her class at the university Outside of speaking for the "I Took the Pledge" group, this was the first time I spoke publicly to a panel or another kind of group. This time my presentation was to college students regarding my diagnosis and experiences.

My ability to speak publicly matured even more to the point that my teachers selected me to address our senior class at graduation. Once in a letter of referral, Deborah Filippelli, one of the "I Took the Pledge" counselors, stated, "... it became apparent Marlon had a special gift as a communicator. At the age of 16, he was able to command the stage in front of audiences of hundreds of teens, as well as adults, and motivate them into action... At 18, he delivered a speech worthy of a professional speaker." Both Deborah and Debbie were instruments used by God to create pivotal moments that redirected my journey.

My life also pivoted positively in non-academic settings while in high school. I was named a McDonald's Corporation top twenty high school senior. I became the first African American class president in my sophomore year. I chose not to run again for president my junior year. I successfully ran for class treasurer instead. During my senior year, I became the school store manager. My decision to run for class treasurer opened the door for the store manager position in my senior year.

My pledge program involvement proved to be an asset for gaining popularity amongst my classmates, which also helped me get elected. People like Louise Lovdahl critiqued my speeches as I prepared for each election campaign. She and Deborah Filippelli were always there to make sure I practiced. Louise and Deborah also knew my audience quite well, making it easier for me to relate. My close peers were additionally instrumental in my campaigns.

I perceived myself as a successful class president because my goal was to advocate for the interests of all students. There was no problem too big or too small to address. I stood for what I believed was right and essential for "ALL" students. I am sure the struggles I faced academically contributed to my empathetic ear for everyone. I often found myself as the connector between well-known, popular students and the class underdogs.

The school store was in a transformation stage during my junior year. An actual store was located in the school cafeteria. I was excited to work as an entrepreneur and manager of the store. I found myself rising early each school day and staying late after school dismissal to ensure the store operations ran smoothly. The store was successful, creating a profitable business model.

———

After the presentation at Debbie's college, I became one of her subjects in her thesis, "Never, Never, Never, Give Up: Resilience Among Individuals with Learning Disabilities." I was referred to as "Martin" in her research. Debbie was that Servant Advocate that released the idea of true resilience and redirection in my life. She made me realize if I could realign the gifts within me, continuing to be resilient along the way, I could go farther than I ever anticipated. In fact, Debbie encouraged me to apply for college, a journey at one point in my life I thought I would never have the opportunity to take. I registered to take the ACTs through a "learning disabilities program, " allowing additional testing time. Not properly preparing myself for the first attempt, I scored an 18 on the second try following laborious self-study.

Debbie's persistence to redirect my journey to get a college education led me through multiple searches for colleges that would enroll students with dyslexia. I finally landed at Carthage College after initially rejecting the opportunity to attend there. Carthage, located in Kenosha, Wisconsin, is a private college affiliated with the Evangelical Lutheran Church in America. Because of becoming an Eagle Scout, Carthage's president highly recommended me.

My journey at Carthage was not an easy one. I chose classes such as psychology that focused on sharing experiences. Additionally, I learned to balance my coursework with discussion-oriented classes. I also used tutorial writing programs, audiobooks on tapes, and a tape recorder during lectures to help me retain the information. I additionally utilized a computer I received through a vocational program to help keep my grades up. I spent four to five hours studying outside of class for every hour I spent in class.

While attending Carthage, I became the vice-president of the Black Student Union in 1992. During that time, African American students sought to define themselves on the campus because Carthage's African American student enrollment had reached an all-time high. I also became socially engaged and actively involved in other areas of college life.

My active social life carried me to the University of Wisconsin in Madison, where I met Dr. Abraham Lincoln Davis, a professor at Morehouse College. A native of Tuskegee, Alabama, Dr. Davis earned his bachelor's in political science from Morehouse, and his master's and Ph.D., in political science from the University of Wisconsin and Ohio State University, respectively. I was intrigued by Dr. Davis and his profound knowledge of Constitutional Law.

During our meeting, Dr. Davis agreed to come and speak to the Black Student Union at Carthage. Since he participated as a research professor in a summer program at the University of Wisconsin, I volunteered to drive Dr. Davis over to Carthage. The journey back to Kenosha was insightful. He shared the differences between attending a private Lutheran College versus attending a Historical Black College. I began wondering what the exposure of attending a Historical Black College would be like for me. By the time I drove Dr. Davis back to the University of Wisconsin, I was enamored.

Later, I called Dr. Davis to see if he could write a letter of recommendation for me to attend Morehouse. This vision of mine may have been seen as farfetched. Even for me, it was beyond my reality. Dr. Davis wrote the letter, and I applied to Morehouse College, an institution dedicated to empowering Black men. I was accepted, which turned out to be another pivotal moment in my life. I believe even now that my acceptance was based on Dr. Davis' reputation. Before leaving for Morehouse, I had just pledged into the renowned Alpha Phi Alpha Fraternity Incorporated at Carthage. While pledging at Carthage, my grades were fine. However, once classes started at Morehouse College, I became overwhelmed because I struggled academically. The same Dyslexia that challenged me all my life took a toll while attending Morehouse. Yet, it introduced me to another crucial turning point. I felt ready to expand my journey again.

While at Morehouse, it was recommended that I be tested again. The new tests carried me on a journey to

Landmark College in Vermont in 1993 for a Summer Program. At that time, Landmark College was the only college in the United States that exclusively enrolled students with learning challenges like dyslexia. Landmark prides itself as "a community designed exclusively for students who learn differently, including students with a learning disability (such as dyslexia), ADHD, autism, or executive function challenges."[1]

Attending Landmark was like finding gold because they met me where I was academically, while providing me opportunities for learning and growth without feeling threatened. Even though it was a challenge, the skills learned at Landmark have carried me through my adult life as well. I began to realize that one semester at Morehouse was a vehicle to redirect me to Landmark. Thus, I had no regrets about attending Morehouse even though I could not stay.

After my summer excursion at Landmark, I came full circle by returning to Carthage College to complete my degree. Carthage welcomed me openly, realizing that further testing identified my academic needs and that I was ready for the challenge. When I returned to Carthage, I was officially in my senior year because I had enough credit hours. I attended as a commuter student, no longer living on campus or embracing the college social life. This return to Carthage is where I had my first

---

1   ©2022 Landmark College. All rights reserved. www.landmark.edu.

spiritual encounter with the Lord. I actually saw myself crossing the stage graduating. That visual experience continued to give me the push and drive to persevere to the end. What seemed like detours in my life were actually the correct paths for me to get where I needed to be to obtain my degree.

Debbie Olufs continued to shadow my progress throughout this journey as she prepared her thesis. Dr. Lisa Bixby, the professor who allowed Debbie to shadow me in her classes at Carthage, was instrumental in getting me hired as an admissions counselor at the University of Arizona International after I graduated. Dr. Bixby relocated to Arizona and accepted a new job at the University of Arizona International, creating another pivotal moment. Aware of my dyslexic challenges, Lisa went from being my professor to becoming a colleague and Servant Advocate for me at the university.

Using the speaking skills gained from junior high school to college made publicly addressing potential students as admissions counselor easy. However, there were some occasions where the report writing requirements of my job were a challenge. I did not let fear hold me back from asking Lisa to proof my reports when needed to make sure my work was done with excellence. Yet, I did not want to become a burden to my colleagues who assisted me. Of course, this was before the availability of the writing tools we now have in the marketplace.

Beyond all those pivotal moments I shared, there are still struggles in my learning styles even today. Even though I have robust attributes as an oral communicator, there are times when I experience moments of shame or uncertainty in my present workplace environment. I wonder if I should share my story with my peers and colleagues. There are other times when I face the frustrations of preparing for an occasion where I must perform a task that requires both oral and written responses. I find myself wondering, "Do my thoughts flow well? Does the information I am presenting sound correct? Will the listener understand what I am trying to say?"

I focus on always remaining ahead of the tasks presented to positively contribute to the team. Mainly since many Human Resource Developments focus on promoting collaboration. Because I am now self-aware of my learning challenges, I seize the moments when I am presented with learning opportunities. I have developed habits as an early riser in the mornings to allow time to process what my day looks like and what specific requirements I will face during the day. When my senior managers request information or status reports, I am well prepared to articulate my response clearly, understanding what is being asked.

Career-wise, I have reached another pivotal moment as a supervisor for the company I presently serve. Yet, even at 50 years old, there are still moments of insecurity. I know preparation is critical, and now as an adult, I understand why Louise Lovdahl spoke those words "practice, practice, practice" to me so many times. However, because I am self-aware of my capabilities, I do not ignore the need to collaborate with my peers to ensure a successful outcome. My goal is to always make sure I have something to bring to the table to contribute to my organization. I plan to always bring better than my "A-game" if that is possible.

From the perspective of a Servant Advocate, it is essential to remember that your mentee facing learning challenges such as dyslexia may experience mental fatigue because they must sometimes go beyond that extra mile to be a team contributor. This is especially true in an adult workplace environment.

With each pivotal moment in my life, I have learned that my struggles are not necessarily the struggles of my Servant Advocate or the people who love me, such as my family. Although they have volunteered to help me on many occasions, I realize that the final push to succeed in every situation is my responsibility.

I now see every pivotal moment as a pivoting moment, the same as one might see a basketball player on the court, pivoting their feet trying to decide which is the best direction to go to make a basket or successful assist.

5

Only YOU can Choose to be a Change Agent

"Jesus answered by telling a story. "There was once a man traveling from Jerusalem to Jericho. On the way he was attacked by robbers. They took his clothes, beat him up, and went off leaving him half-dead. Luckily, a priest was on his way down the same road, but when he saw him he angled across to the other side. Then a Levite religious man showed up; he also avoided the injured man. A Samaritan traveling the road came on him. When he saw the man's condition, his heart went out to him. He gave him first aid, disinfecting and bandaging his wounds. Then he lifted him onto his donkey, led him to an inn, and made him comfortable." (Luke 10: 30 – 35a Message)

nly you can choose to become a Servant Advocate and agent of change in someone's life who needs assistance. The Samaritan in this story was the third person to encounter the injured gentleman on the side of the road. The other two passersby chose to cross over to the other side and ignore the man's condition.

The purpose of sharing my story is to encourage you to not be the person that turns away from a life of purpose just because there are challenges to overcome to succeed. There are numerous reasons to get SOAPY as a Servant Advocate and make a difference in the life of a child, family member, colleague, friend, or stranger that crosses your path.

One valid reason is that the gifts and talents of many people are lying dormant and unnoticed because when given the opportunity, we choose to cross to the other side of the road. There are raw talents that need to be developed in people like me who face daily academic learning challenges.

It is said that graveyards are the wealthiest places on the earth because of the untapped talent and gifts that have been buried there. Relative to becoming a Servant Advocate, the one thing that can rob graveyards world-wide of that untapped talent is YOUR time.

The encourager within me says to you that it is possible to encounter hidden talent like the "Les Browns" of the world. Les, one of the world's leading motivational speakers and former multi-term state representative in

Ohio, was declared "educable mentally retarded" in grade school.[1]

The encourager in me thinks of people like Henry Thurman, Bill Ennis, and Louise Lovdahl, who chose not to look the other way. They committed to nurturing the untapped talent within a young black man who some considered "special." The encourager in me thinks of Debbie Olufs, who persisted in identifying my academic challenges while telling me I could pursue higher education opportunities.

Because of these Servant Advocates, I have hope within me that I have been and will continue to be the change agent in others' lives. I believe that the same way Jeremiah 29:11 applies to my life, it applies to others who have similar struggles related to dyslexia. "For I know the plans I have for you, declares the Lord, plans to prosper you and not to harm you, plans to give you hope and a future." (Jeremiah 29:11)

The genuine change agents are the people who desire to see mankind in a more excellent state. I, like these people, believe in a better tomorrow. We choose to rise up as Servant Advocates even though we know our missions are only temporary and our lives will not last forever.

————

As the mentee of the incredible Servant Advocates I

1   Les Brown. https://lesbrown.com. Viewed 2022.

shared about, I knew there would be struggles along my journey. But I still wanted to become the best Marlon Harmon possible. I wanted to share my story because of the trials I battled through. My story serves as an example of what you, a Servant Advocate, can do for others if you choose to accept the assignment. The Servant Advocate inside me says that you can, and you will take my challenge. Looking at where I have come from, you can make an incredible difference as the next change agent for someone battling their dyslexic world.

I realize that my journey has not ended, and I will encounter other obstacles. I have desires and dreams I want to achieve in my career. Even as an adult, I also recognize that I still need Servant Advocates to help me along the way in my career and in the advancement of opening doors for others, like myself. But I believe I can and will make it to the next level. These new levels don't always have to be enormous. They may be considered small steps but attainable ones. I may be a supervisor right now, but my eyes are fixed on becoming a senior supervisor and later a superintendent.

My dreams as a Servant Advocate have expanded regarding my ability to help others since writing this book. After this book, I dream of other books within me ready to be written. Thanks to technology and new Servant Advocates, that dream is possible. I gained a new reality of endurance, enabling me to have greater patience for new mentees I will encounter.

I recognize being a Servant Advocate is not for everyone. Not everyone will take the steps needed to become a Servant Advocate. Not every Servant Advocate will have unlimited amounts of patience.

I also recognize that some potential mentees are not a good fit and will not accept the outreached hand of a Servant Advocate. But when we, as Servant Advocates, do our part, we realize that there will be reservations and a point of personal discovery that the mentee must experience before they accept us. We understand there are growing pains that come along with growth. Yet, we remember there are still opportunities for growth and development of the mentees if given a chance.

I don't know the exact outcomes of other mentees on their journeys. But I know my outcome is a living testimony of what can happen when someone chooses to become a change agent as a Servant Advocate.

Even though I faced tough times, I have no regrets from my childhood experiences as a mentee. Revisiting some of those experiences as an adult, I see a clearer picture of why I couldn't understand learning situations. These pictures are based on the new discoveries I have made about myself. I am at the place now where I can say with peace, "This is the hand I have been given. I choose to make the best of it." Realizing that statement in the deepest part of my inner self makes a difference in planning my journey forward. This decision sets me apart from feeling like I have to be "like Mike" or anyone else. I now realize I just have to be Marlon. Thus, my hope is that every mentee that I serve comes to the realization that they only have to be themselves, that fearfully, wonderfully human being God made.

———

The saying, "no man is an island," holds true in Servant Advocacy. Whenever I reflect on my journey, I recognize others were involved in my successes as advocates.

"No man is an island, entire of itself; every man is a piece of the continent, a part of the main. If a clod be washed away by the sea, Europe is the less, as well as if a promontory were, as well as if a manor of thy friend's or of thine own were: Any man's death diminishes me, because I am involved in mankind, and therefore never send to know for whom the bells tolls; it tolls for thee."[2]

I understand I am needed on this earth to serve as an advocate. Thus, I choose to take the time to identify those along my path who need advocacy. I seek to find the connections that say to a person in need, "We can work together. We can make new discoveries that will elevate your life and create success. We can also handle the

---

2   John Donne, No man is an island – A selection from the prose quote. https://allpoetry.com/No-man-is-an-island. View 2022.

setbacks and challenges that we will encounter." The word resiliency is defined as "the capacity to recover quickly from difficulties; toughness."[3] I look for opportunities to demonstrate resiliency as I seek to be that change agent in another person's life.

I believe that from birth, I was destined to live a life of resiliency because my mother was resilient. My mother was a hard worker, and even though she lacked specific skillsets, she never quit trying and striving for better. Reflecting, I wonder if my mother had encountered a Servant Advocate early in her life, would things have been different.

There is always rigorous competition in the marketplace and in my industry. I believe leaders have a greater charge to mentor, coach, and motivate the people they serve in an organization to draw the most from them.

Presently, I am responsible for thirty people in our organization during any given time. Based on their training requirements, some will remain longer in the organization than others. Upon successfully completing the training requirements, some will move forward with new opportunities. While I must encourage others, who did not fare well to keep trying and consider a retest. Some will also choose to walk away and move on to something else because they feel the challenge is too great.

I realize that everyone brings something different to the

---

3   LEXICO powered by Oxford. https://www.lexico.coom/en/definition/resilience. Viewed 2022.

table. My responsibility is to walk alongside each person to help bring their very best out. That means I should know if a trainee needs a Servant Advocate to stand in the gap for them. Their positive outcomes benefit them and our company, making us a thriving force against our competitors. I am not afraid to share that my testimony also includes multiple retests with those who encounter failure. The key is to never give up.

———

I liken my life as a Servant Advocate and mentee to an experience I shared in 2021 with my brother, Vincent. He and I took a 75-mile bike ride in the Arizona desert. Once starting the journey, we realized it would take longer than we anticipated. We also discovered that greater endurance was needed for the bike trip than planned.

"During the last part of the journey, I realized the physical tank in my body was empty."[4] Within five miles of our destination, I knew my energy level was at zero, and there was no reserve left in me. The only thing I could do at that point was visualize making it back to our vehicle. I could hear the thoughts in my brain say, "the car, the car, the car." I knew if I focused on my

---

4   Dr. Amanda Goodson and Daniel L. Scott, Jr., Resilient: A key to being Brilliant, USA. ©2021 by Amanda Goodson and Daniel L. Scott, Jr.

final destination, I could "will" myself to the end of the journey, so I continued paddling.

As a Servant Advocate, there will be times when we reach the place where we think there is no more hope for our mentee. We have paddled all we can, and we are emotionally and physically bottomed out. At that point, we must rely on the vision of being a change agent of promise to those we are assisting.

We have a responsibility to meet people where they are. Whether we are leaders in the marketplace, an academic setting, or clergy in the ministry, we must recognize the need and accept the challenge as a Servant Advocate. From the point of acceptance, the journey begins.

Through Lincoln Elementary School, the Ennis family met me where I was. Louise Lovdahl met me where I was emotionally and academically at Lincoln Junior High School. Marv Warter met me at an infection point in my life, demonstrated patience, and developed and coached me to further my journey.

Debbie Olufs met me where I was and used the opportunity to start me on a journey to higher education. The professors at various colleges and universities on my journey met me where I was and helped me achieve my goals of earning a bachelor's and master's degree.

The life of Servant Advocacy may require "baby steps" when working with a mentee experiencing dyslexic challenges. Whether in the marketplace or ministry, we must exhibit the patience necessary to get to know the people who labor amongst us to determine their needs. This means there may be less sleep from time to time. It also means that we must lead with an actual open-door policy. If someone in the organization feels they need assistance to overcome their challenges, they must know they have the freedom to ask without demoralization.

I want to share the following information for the parent who feels their child's opportunities for success are limited because of dyslexia. According to an article written by Jillian Petrova[5], successful dyslexics noted these advantages they experienced that contributed to their achievements.

- **An awe-inspiring ability to remember details of a story or event.** This capability "may help improve your memory and help integrate contextual information better."[6]
- **Exceptional puzzle-solving abilities.** This capability demonstrates the ability to solve complex problems. "Many dyslexics thrive in an environment that allows and fosters simultaneous thinking in which ideas are connected via different routes than a straight line."[7] Additionally, dyslexics

5   Jillian Petrova, "The Many Strengths of Dyslexics," My Dyslexia Help Success Starts Here, http://dyslexiahelp.umich.edu/dyslexics/learn-about-dyslexia/what-is-dyslexia/the-many-strengths-of-dyslexics. January 10, 2022.
6   Jillian Petrova, Ibid.
7   Jillian Petrova, Ibid.

tend to "use logical reasoning," exhibiting dynamic critical thinking skills.

- **Superb three-dimensional reasoning.** According to scientists at the University of East London, "young dyslexics are excellent at remembering a virtual environment when compared to non-dyslexics."[8]
- **Exceptional oral communicators.** Although dyslexics experience various reading challenges, they demonstrate a keen ability to read personalities, listen effectively, and connect well with others orally. Thus, giving them a stage can produce exceptional results.
- **Out-of-the-box thinkers.** Dyslexics are known for their vivid imaginations, demonstrating the ability to comprehend abstract ideas and foster originality.
- **The ability to empathize.** Due to the challenges dyslexics face daily, they are likely to be more empathetic to the needs of others facing difficulty.

I found many of these characteristics to be true in my life. Because I demonstrated these capabilities, I have experienced much success in the marketplace. I also encourage leaders in the marketplace to note these remarkable capabilities of dyslexics, meaning don't prejudge an opportunity to unleash greatness in your organization through someone with dyslexia.

Parents and leaders in the marketplace and community,

---

8   Jillian Petrova, Ibid.

I strongly encourage you to remember the following notes about dyslexics:

The traditional forms of dyslexia may not be every dyslexic's experience. The challenges I experience are not just about how written words appear to me. I don't see words backward. My experience is more of a language processing challenge. When I transition from oral communication to written communication, the words in my head lose their suffix.

Every individual's experience is different, so get to know that individual and their needs.

Remember to meet the dyslexic (your child or mentee) where they are. Become their first Servant Advocate who gives them a voice to receive academic and professional assistance.

Only you can choose to become a change agent in the life of someone facing challenges from dyslexia. While writing this book, I received a new certification from The Narrative Initiative (TNI). This organization "catalyzes durable narrative change in order to make equity and social justice common sense."[9] I hope to use this certification as a facilitator to invite other leaders to come to the table and discuss how we can become better change agents and Servant Advocates in the marketplace and community.

I also desire to use a similar platform for dyslexics to share and express themselves relative to the complexities

---

9   Narrativeinitiative.org. 2022.

of their everyday lives. No, I am not a psychiatrist or psychologist. I am Marlon Harmon, a man who continues to triumph over the challenges of living in a dyslexic world. I am a man who has chosen to become a Servant Advocate and change agent in the lives of others who are also ready to triumph.

The Servant Advocate Challenge:

Now that you have read my story, I hope that you are ready to get SOAPY as a Servant Advocate in the lives of one of the more than seven million people faced with learning challenges like dyslexia. Getting SOAPY is essential because being a Servant Advocate means there will be times when your hands get dirty (figuratively) through the difficulties of helping someone achieve beyond the challenges of dyslexia. The goals of getting SOAPY are simple, as provided below.

S	Become a **Servant Advocate** for adults and children with learning disabilities.
O	Expect an **Outcome** that changes lives.
A	Take the **Action** necessary to make a difference in the lives of those who need you.
P	Create **Pivotal** moments that redirect the recipient's journey through the challenges faced.
Y	Only **You** can choose to be a change agent in the lives of others.

I extend this challenge to you because as a Servant Advocate, you can become the person who advocates for those who cannot fight or stand in the gap for themselves. You can be that person who places themselves in the shoes of those suffering from learning disabilities to feel what they feel and to hold up their arms when those who need assistance feel like giving up.

Dr. Martin Luther King, Jr. is memorably known for this remark regarding servanthood.

If you want to be important-wonderful. If you want to be recognized-wonderful. If you want to be great-wonderful. But recognize that he who is greatest among you shall be your servant. That's a new definition of greatness. By giving that definition of greatness it means that everybody can be great, because everybody can serve. You don't have to have a college degree to serve. You don't have to make your subject and your verb agree to serve. You don't have to know about Plato and Aristotle to serve. You don't have to know Einstein's theory of relativity to serve. You don't have to know the second theory of thermodynamics in physics to serve. You only need a heart full of grace, a soul generated by love. And you can be that servant.[1]

It's your time to become that change agent as a Servant Advocate!

Email me and let me know how you have chosen to make a difference as a Servant Advocate.

marlonbtcn2020@gmail.com or www.btcngroup.com

1   Dr. Martin Luther King, "Drum Major Instinct," Stanford University, https://kinginstitute. stanford.edu/encyclopedia/drum-major-instinct. February 4, 1968.

The Underdog Must Become the Big Dog

Rick was in his forties with a thin, narrow build and a strong, imposing presence. Yet it was apparent that he didn't have great self-esteem. He didn't feel like he was in the right place at the right time.

In my eight months of interaction with Rick as his supervisor and as a servant advocate, we developed a relationship in which he identified his struggles—and they were many. He acknowledged how some of his past challenges, like being incarcerated and having addictions to alcohol and other substances, were very difficult. Especially when he occasionally revisited that chemical dependency, putting himself at risk of jeopardizing his employment. Worse, he could lose his wife and his children.

As I got to know Rick as a person and as an employee, I constantly assured him that he was significant and added value to my team. That became important to both of us as he continued to learn and demonstrate his competency at work. Near the close of our brief time together, I watched him move from an OM4 to an OM5 level employee in our industry. That promotion is anything but simple. It required specialized training and testing that he truly struggled with.

Question was, would he be able to overcome and succeed in life as well as at work?

As a youngster, Rick was a rebel rouser. He got in trouble quite a bit and actually enjoyed getting into mischief. Over time, he was charged with possession and use of drugs as well as intent to sell. He was incarcerated several times, and he shared with me that he was supposed to have been incarcerated for life. Yet when we began working together, it seemed God had something greater for him.

His drinking started at a younger than normal age because of the crowd he was involved with. Just as I learned as a youngster in middle school and high school, alcohol is the gateway drug to other drugs, and that certainly proved to be the case for Rick. The thing about addiction is that it never ends. It requires the discipline and resilience to seek help when it is needed and called for, for your own success. Rick shared that there were times when he needed to be clear of both alcohol and drugs. During our engagement with each other, he once admitted that he had returned to drinking after getting into a rough spot in his personal life. That's a usual tendency for individuals who then have to keep themselves from falling into a deeper pit with other substances until, in many cases, they manipulate their situation, their family, and their story to chase after that next top-of-the-world high, so they can feel better. I continued to encourage Rick to fight hard for his youngest daughter and for his teenage daughter who would perhaps be influenced by peer pressure. I told him that the woes of life could come knocking on her door if she didn't have anyone to depend on. I used such scenarios as instruments to remind him why he should stay the course and ask for help.

Prior to my departure from the Climax Molybdenum Company that operates an open pit molybdenum mine in Colorado where Rick served under my leadership, he began to lose focus. He struggled with being attentive to the tasks at hand. Details, such as the recording of data or items missed when checking for pH levels or turbidity in the water to be tested and treated before exiting the plant and being released to the community, had to be corrected. At the same time, Rick attempted to lean on his family for strength and be responsible to them, but there was evidence in his mood, his attitude, and his behavior that he was really at a place of tremendous struggle. His approach to our conversations shifted away from positive aspects of his family life, such as how his oldest daughter was doing in school or how he and his mom had such a tremendous relationship, to talking about the difficulties in his marriage and the negative influence his father's alcohol and drug laden lifestyle had on him. His mother had witnessed Rick's journey from the start, from watching her son find trouble and weave in and out of it to seeing him make a profession for change to the place where he became a strong, responsible, married man who purchased a home to help protect and care for his family. She was truly his first servant advocate. She truly believed in her son, always met him where he was in life, and encouraged him to do better and improve himself.

I held on with Rick as his servant advocate as he dealt with these challenges at home and at work. When Rick originally started with the company, he was a training operator learning the roles of a water technician. He moved to the OM1 level, becoming more responsible for specific details of the job including the personal accountability of showing up every day when he was scheduled. He progressed to OM2, then OM3. I met him at OM4 and on the cusp of being promoted to the highest paying bracket in the company at the OM5 level. One of his responsibilities was to acquire two water licenses that would be honored by the state showing that he understood potable water and how it is treated in the workplace all the way to advanced levels of treatment.

It was initially a chore to inspire and motivate him to the next level. Like myself, he had a very real fear of taking tests. Part of it was his learning style. He could go through his day-to-day process and understand the job with rote memory to the point he could do it with his eyes closed, but testing felt like a boot camp-type experience. The tests are timed, not for the sake of speed, but for competency, yet that time pressure element had a way of startling him. He struggled in that environment.

I helped Rick as best as I could—and he did overcome and succeed! He achieved OM5. When I left the organization, I went to leadership and said, "This individual truly demonstrates competency and the knowledge," so I was a little instrumental in the outcome.

When I last engaged with Rick, transitions were occurring, and he knew that one of his biggest cheerleaders was not going to be around. He was a little discouraged and concerned about the unknown. As I stayed in touch via phone and video calls, I saw Rick once more struggling and plummeting a little into addiction. As of this writing, he has gone to rehab, is on the mend, and is back at work, eager and ready to help the next person coming through. However, he is also going through a divorce and continuing to fight hard to keep his kids. He is sharing custody of his two children from that marriage and of his oldest daughter from a previous relationship.

Is Rick succeeding? Yes. Has that success come with its setbacks? That answer is also "yes." But Rick is moving forward and onward, and it was my responsibility and privilege to help him. As I did, I was able to "Lather Up" and get SOAPY with Rick as his (S) Servant Advocate by encountering him, getting to know him, and meeting him where he was in his life, so I could help him get to where he needed to go. The importance of lathering up is to get the dirt off, and the lather is the cleaning agent that results from our servant advocacy efforts. Getting to know an individual and having the courage to meet them where they are is *the vital step* to determining how to get them where they need to go. That's what we do as servant advocates.

Rick was able to Expect an Outcome (O) as he began studying and training to get the license and certification that the company's line of progression required for the next possible promotion from OM4 to OM5. As he passed the classes and earned points toward that certification, his expectation for that outcome grew. This took additional time in conjunction with his normal work duties, but he did it—and as his servant advocate, I helped him along and enjoyed seeing my expectation for his outcome expand as a result. Sharing in that outcome is just one of the joys and benefits of servant advocacy.

Next, Rick did what he had to do to Take the Action (**A**) of being at work on time. It was huge for him to be disciplined in that way, as well as to be accountable for scheduling around moments when he couldn't be there. An unplanned work interruption occurred when he suffered an abruption in his midsection one morning and was rushed to the hospital. I recall working overnight and heading directly from work to the hospital to visit him. Rick didn't know I was coming, and he appreciated that I showed up to check on him and his family. I was authentic about that and shared with my team members and my bosses that I did it because it was who I am and that he is a part of my crew and our work family. That reshaped our relational dynamic in his eyes. We moved from the work relationship to something deeper. I contacted his wife, who was pregnant at the time, to see if there was anything she needed. I followed up throughout the two days he was hospitalized after his procedure. There was a moment when the doctor came into his room while I was there. I asked if I should leave, and he said I didn't have to go anywhere. Rick told the doctor that I was his supervisor and had come all the way there to check on him.

That type of personal involvement became an outcome shifter for him, and it added to his desire to be accountable and take the necessary actions to achieve what he wanted to accomplish at the workplace. As servant advocates, we want to Create Pivotal Moments (**P**) to redirect others through their challenges, and that proved to be my moment with Rick.

Finally, knowing that Only You (**Y**) can choose to be a change agent, Rick took that moment and the entirety of our time together to propel himself toward the promotion he desired. He has begun to believe in himself, and he knows that what he wants to achieve is indeed within his reach.

My engagement with Rick meant a lot for me as a servant advocate. Simply having the opportunity to see someone develop, grow, and shift was fuel for me and, really, it's what "be the change now" represents. We can talk about a lot of things, but what are we going to *do*? I saw something tremendously special in this gentleman's life, and I believe that anyone would have counted him as the underdog. He had served time. He had tattoos around his skull and neck. The stereotypical viewpoint of society would easily conclude, "Oh, this person is a thug or a gangbanger," finding ways to count him out. Yet that's why I believe in the SOAPY opportunities that we're given as servant advocates. I had to lather up and come side-by-side with Rick, know who he was, meet him where he was at, help reshape him, and shine a light on the path that was already there for him. That provided him with the inspiration to grow personally and inspire his family. Rick encouraged me to remember that it's not how we start but where we end up, and how we make it happen, that matters. Servant advocacy has to be done in a big way. There were times with Rick when I could've easily checked myself out. After leaving that company, I could've chosen not to stay in touch with Rick. I didn't do either of those things. I stayed involved. As of this writing, Rick remains in Colorado while I reside part-time in California, but Rick and I remain steadfast friends, accountability partners, and are still reaching for the stars, even as we go through similar situations with our respective families.

———

Another underdog I have lathered up and become SOAPY with as a servant advocate is Roeline "Ru" Hansen. A native of Namibia who currently lives and works in South Africa, she has a heart of gold and is taking it to the next level as founder and visionary director of Elevate Education Solutions. Its mission is to transform educational environments for youngsters through accessible, impactful resources and development services that elevate the potential of every learner, teacher, and leader. Ru's organization is designed to create a self-sustaining educational ecosystem where every supply purchase is directly reinvested into the growth of schools and communities in South Africa. Many schools there struggle to get quality educational supplies affordably. No reinvestment models exist, so once money leaves the school, it doesn't return. Yet teachers, learners, and parents need support programs that nurture their youngsters' growth beyond academics. Ru aims to provide those programs— lathering up and being SOAPY for youth not only in small communities, but an entire nation.

Ru grew up in a very divided social and political environment, yet she recognizes herself as a global citizen dedicated to making a difference. She and I met during our undergraduate years at Carthage College in Kenosha, Wisconsin after she had been selected as one of 100 Namibian students to receive a scholarship from the Lutheran World Federation. That opportunity opened doors to new learning environments and cultural experiences in the United States. Like so many of the foreign students that I connected with at Carthage, Ru and I became close friends and remained that way after she transferred to a college in California. For over a decade, Ru trained in healing arts (message, yoga, and tai chi), deepening her connection with self-awareness and nurturing her passion for holistic wellness.

Ru is a Christ follower who is motivated, excited, and operates with a high level of excellence. She found herself consumed with a burning passion to bring awareness of educational opportunities to teachers and learners in her nation. She asked for my opinion on the name of her organization, what I thought about her vision, and how I could support her in her endeavor. Today, Ru and I speak by video chat each month and continue to encourage one another on our journeys and in our shared passion for the development of people. We talk about what others have done for us, sometimes through prayer and financial resources, so that we can continue to hit our benchmarks and dream the bigger dreams for what we want to do in people's lives. I continue to benefit and learn from her energy and enthusiasm to meet people where they are and help them.

I see Ru as an underdog through her unwavering commitment to her vision. As a female she has had to courageously face and overcome gender and race obstacles to impact others. Her journey began in Kalkrand, a rural town in southern Namibia, where she went to A.A. Denk Primary and attended various boarding schools starting when she was 12 years of age. A mentor recognized her potential, and she was eventually accepted at Concordia College in Windhoek. That's where she was nurtured by dedicated educators and supportive peers, cultivating invaluable friendships that deepened her resilience and laid the foundation for her future endeavors in the United States.

It was in 2009, during a Native American sweat ceremony, that she received a simple message: "give birth." She began seeing each learning experience as a gift she was gathering to share with others. The following year, she returned to Namibia. She received another message in 2011. "Arise, child," it declared. "I have dreams to manifest through you."

Ru taught in various regions (Erongo, Otjozondjupa, Khomas, Oshana, and Hardap), ultimately transitioning into wellness leadership at safari lodges (Habitas Namibia, Motswari, Thornybush, and the Royal Ingwe River Lodge), forging a path aligned with her calling and vision. The emergence of Elevate Education Solutions symbolizes her journey, creating pathways for impactful and sustainable learning experiences. Her organization is so much larger than herself, but she lost one of her closest advocates, her mother, about a decade before its development. Still, Ru persists determinedly as a **(S)** Servant Advocate because her dream embodies the ideal of "no one left behind." As she puts it, "Potential is not defined by geography. It is awakened by those who recognize it." Her vision expands far beyond a specific group of people to believe, as I do, that everyone deserves a spot among those who would become servant advocates for humanity in general.

Ru is positioned to Expect an Outcome **(O)** because she knows that without proper learning and training, it is much more difficult for youngsters and others to advance in a changing, technical world. She wants everyone to be able to gain, contribute, and find their place. "Sometimes purpose moves you," she said, "so you can learn every part of the ecosystem you are called to transform." Due to the many years of Apartheid in southern Africa and the challenges of having to deal with sectors of people who think more or less of themselves and others, we know that all practitioners and participants in a divided society need to know that they, too, are significant. People like Ru Take the Action (**A**) by inviting everyone to the table to teach, learn, and encourage others to become change agents. They may have been counted out in the past, but we are assured that they can be counted back in and go from being the underdog to the big dog so that we can all win. "Closed doors are not rejections," Ru says. "They are redirections toward the door you are meant to build yourself."

I look at Ru's life and how she started out geared toward health and wellness, then expanded into learning and teaching, as the transformative model for how she will continue to Create Pivotal Moments (**P**) through what she is aiming to do for herself and others. Knowing that Only You (**Y**) can choose to be a change agent, Ru is making herself the "why" for the learners, teachers, and leaders she is serving in a troubled part of the world. She developed a vision and worked diligently to solicit for and unfold all of the proper support and resources to launch her organization as an eager and willing servant advocate. Ru exemplifies this persona. She knows it begins and ends with her.

For all of us who can find ourselves in a place of feeling down or low on our faith, Ru's story inspires us to take a selfless, personal look at ourselves, recapture our hope, and rekindle our faith. Like Ru, all of us have the ability to create something out of nothing to make an incredible difference and leave a lasting legacy.

———

The final underdog I'd like to share with you is one I know all too well—yet am just beginning to *really* get to know him in an entirely new and significant way.

His name is Marlon Harmon.

Me.

Throughout the earlier years of my own personal development, I was consumed with the assumption that I was doing the right thing. I found and served in those little niches where people needed the support of a servant advocate. Later, I realized that I needed to revisit those who stood in my corner because I may have digressed in my own personal journey. I still needed their advocacy for my own growth and to continue to develop. I needed their support at specific junctures and moments as a servant advocate. Now, in spite of the challenges I have faced and will still face, I am triumphing through the recognition that it is okay to revisit those people and moments. It is okay to reset. It is okay to reflect and use what I learned as benchmarks to pivot back into a position of strength. As I matured, still a young man, I came to realize that disconnections happened along the journey regardless of whether or not I was paying attention. In recent years, personal challenges have revealed that I became a little complacent, taking for granted the things that came naturally.

Now, I am reflecting on my life while I complete this book, and I can see that my ability to be a servant advocate has diminished somewhat. I realize that a little bit of the flame died down as I became comfortable, perhaps from being married and having a family, being focused on work, or a combination of both. As a result, I lost perspective on the bigger things and on my space in this universe to reach out and help others.

The one God-given attribute that I believe has been the cornerstone of my life is patience. I operate in calmness as my way of existence. Yet over the last couple of years, I have struggled internally, feeling like I was not contributing or that I was always wrong as I navigated a challenging relationship at home. Through some tough, tragic situations, including the breakup of my family, I had to be willing to confess my own truths, errors, and follies. In my own imperfections and deficits, I lost the ability to be hopeful—and the spark that I had when I birthed this book was no longer there.

As I revisit *Triumphing Through My Dyslexic World* and write this last chapter, I have shared the stories of two people who have truly become a brother and a sister from another mother. In the process, I am rekindling the flame once again. I am ready to lather up again and willing to get dirty—not only for those around me that I meet in my workplace and elsewhere, but for myself. I need to be as agile as possible. I need to get in a posture to keep hope alive and never waver with the time God has blessed me with on this earth. My desire is to always be an available advocate, always ready to pivot, always poised to respond to the call to action knowing that there is going to be an expected outcome!

As I made one of the hardest decisions of my adult life, closing off something that I thought would be forever while losing friends and extended family members along the way, I have determined to remain the person that God birthed inside of me. The person He knew when He formed me inside my mother's womb. The person made for such a time as this.

Only I can lather up.

Only I can be SOAPY.

Only I can make a definitive difference.

It's true. Advocates get tired. Advocates become exhausted. People change. Life changes. But we have to be willing to adapt, look at ourselves, clean our own hands, and be ready to continue going into the larger society where we have been called to work and serve.

It is time for us to realize and accept that the underdog must become the big dog.

Contact Marlon at:

marlonbtcn2020@gmail.com